Dog-ku

Very Clever Haikus
Cleverly Written by
Very Clever Dogs

Dog-ku

Steve D. Marsh

Thomas Dunne Books / St. Martin's Griffin ≈ New York

THOMAS DUNNE BOOKS
An Imprint of St. Martin's Press

www.thomasdunnebooks.com
www.stmartins.com

Design by Susan Walsh

Library of Congress Cataloging-in-Publication Data

Marsh, Steve D.
  Dog-ku : very clever haikus cleverly written by very clever dogs / Steve D. Marsh.—1st ed.
      p. cm.
  ISBN-13: 978-0-312-37714-4
  ISBN-10: 0-312-37714-2
  1. Dogs—Poetry. 2. Haiku, American. I. Title.

  PS3613.A7699 D64 2008
  811'.6—dc22

                                                    2007039767

First Edition: November 2008

10 9 8 7 6 5 4 3 2 1

Contents

Contents

Confessions of an Accidental Dog Whisperer

I'm not crazy, or at least not in that way. I know dogs don't talk. I know ESP doesn't exist, or at least I know I don't have it. But there I was one day, back in 1997, out in the backyard, picking rhubarb for a pie, when I distinctly heard from directly behind me, "Hey, I've got an idea."

Thinking I had been alone, I turned and was surprised to find no one there—no one except Zac, my (at the time) two-and-a-half-year-old Black Lab–Rhodesian Ridgeback cross. He looked at me with eagerness, maybe even earnestness. But I attributed the words to be nothing more than the background chatter that goes on inside an idle human mind, and I turned back to my rhubarb duties.

Almost immediately, I heard, "Hey! I said, I've got an idea."

Dog-ku

Molly

Again, I turned to see only Zac, but this time it seemed that something about his usually soft brown eyes implied more than simple earnestness. He seemed to have a little irritation mixed in as well, like he was dealing with a creature of slightly diminished capacity, and he was on the edge of worn patience. "I want to write some poems," I heard. And Zac's head seemed to move in sync with the appropriate emphasis of the words. At that moment, I knew I *was* crazy . . . or it was still the '60s . . . or I needed medication . . . or, maybe, Zac was talking to me psychically.

Tentatively, I said out loud, since I didn't know how to project through ESP, "What kind of poems?"

"I'm thinking something pithy. Short. Truthful. But in form. Nothing says truth like the discipline of form."

"You mean like sonnets or villanelles?"

"No, even shorter."

"Ah, limericks!" I guessed, now immersed in the conversation and willing to set aside that I was likely suffering some kind of psychic break with reality.

"No, nobody reads limericks anymore. I want some-

3

thing that will reach the masses." Zac turned from me and seemed to pace, engrossed in thought. "I think I want to write a series of haiku."

I protested, "But no one in America reads haiku either. Haiku isn't even a form with much of a history in English."

And, of course, about then I realized the absurdity of the argument I was having with my dog. It was also true that no one in America reads poems written by dogs. It's not like critics could resist the use of the word "doggerel" in making a review. My responses became dogged. I trotted out additional arguments.

But Zac remained unswayed.

"Write this down," he said.

I remained incredulous.

"No, really, write this down. You can't expect me to do it." Zac stood feigning additional patience, while I put away my rhubarb knife. We went back in the house, I put the rhubarb in the sink and looked for writing materials.

"You know, this whole syllable counting thing would have been easier if you hadn't removed my thumbs," Zac grumbled.

"Those weren't thumbs; those were dew claws and the vet said you'd be happier without them." I protested.

"Easy for him to say. Did he still have his thumbs when he said that?"

I knew where this conversation was going to end up. I wondered how long until he was going to make me feel guilty for neutering him. Whether it was my guilty feelings or if he simply let me off the hook, he said, "Write this down."

The paperboy comes.
He wants to murder us all!
Bark! Bark! Bark! Bark! Bark!

I was astounded. It was a masterful first attempt (for a dog) I thought. It fit the 5-7-5 syllable form. It seemed to capture a single moment in time. It conveyed a great deal about the emotional state of the charged moment. Each line stood on its own in its own emotional space. And, in typical American amendment to the form, it contained a punch line in the final line. All of the ele-

ments of the renewed and amended American form of the haiku were in place. And this from a two-and-a-half-year-old Lab-Ridgeback.

"That's 18 in dog years, don't forget," Zac interjected.

And thus began Zac's literary career. He is nearly eleven and half years old now (that's over 80 in those dog years) and his mind is still sharp. And even though his night vision is plagued by worsening cataracts, he remains clear headed and mentally alert, despite having lost a step or two in the flat-out run. Just the other day he offered up this one:

> Dry dog food is hard.
> Yet my old teeth are harder.
> Canned food is for cats.

I presume he will remain a stoic to the end.

What follows is a commentary on his art and life from America's first dog of literature, as channeled through me. I am honored to bring this to the world's literate audiences.

6

I should make one final comment on dog channeling. Some of these poems have come from other dogs. Some are offered by our German Shepherd–Lab cross, E.D. Zac and E.D. actually released a small volume of these poems through The Wordsmith Press and worked their way through obedience school on those proceeds. Other haiku come from many dogs I have known and who have entrusted me with their artistic contributions to the genre. Special thanks to the following contributors of more than one or two random poems:

Belle, a fat Beagle
Harley, a wiry Pit Bull cross
Tio, a Dalmatian
Hawk, an English Sheepdog–Bouvier cross

Although some of these early dog poets have crossed over, their contributions to art live on.

—Steve D. Marsh, Accidental Dog Channeler
March 19, 2007

Zac and E.D.

Portrait of the Dog as a Young Artist

Hello. My name is "Zac," although that is not my whole name and it was not my first name.

I was born on November 10, 1995, to a kind Labrador Retriever with soft brown eyes. We lived on a farm in rural Washtenaw County, Michigan. My father was a Rhodesian Ridgeback who had jumped his fence a time or two and I have inherited his haircut. It has earned me respect in my lifetime. There were four of us back then, myself and my three sisters. Only I had the Ridgeback markings along my backbone. The young boy on the farm named me Bear. I suppose I was a little round back then and bigger than my sisters. Mom was a good provider. There were eight feeding stations: one each for my sisters, and five for me.

But one day, Boss and Mrs. Boss came to the farm. I remember Mrs. Boss was wearing a beautiful red wool

coat. Folks say dogs are color blind, but they are wrong. I loved that red coat. It was the same color as Mom's collar. It made me feel at home. I slept on that coat in Mrs. Boss's lap all the way into town.

Boss and Mrs. Boss took me home to their children. It was Christmas Eve. Hey, I don't make this stuff up! They were both English teachers and they spent two days trying to find a good literary name for me. But I puzzled them. I loved food. They had to find a literary name that acknowledged my first love. And women. I loved women, too. There is nothing better than really getting to "nose" a woman. And then they struck upon it. They named me Honoré de Balzac. Great writer, great lover, great eater. It was a perfect name and one I am proud to bear to this day, or that is to say, I should have been proud if they had not truncated it so badly.

First, there were a few (really not more than a few dozen) "accidents" on the floor. I would make a mistake, and promise not to do it again (and I really meant not to do it again), but soon, I'd make another mistake.

10

And another. And another. It didn't take long for Boss to say that there was no Honor in my promises and I became just "de Balzac." And then the "de" went away. It was just easier to say "Balzac." And for several weeks, my name was Balzac. Then one fateful day, Boss took me to the veterinarian, for what he called a "minor" procedure, and when I came home, I was just "Zac." No more "Balz." And so I have remained for the rest of my life.

That operation was intended to adjust my attitude and to keep me closer to home. In some ways it worked. It permitted me to focus more on my art and to work with fewer distractions. I'm not certain it was worth the tradeoff, but the tradeoff was made nonetheless. It taught me an important lesson. Less is more.

Sometime during the early summer of my third year, late adolescence for a dog, I struck upon the idea of being a poet. And I would not be one of those frilly, pretentious poets like at the University. (We lived in Ann Arbor at that time.) I decided to be a poet that told the

truth in the language of real Americans. I would tell the innermost feelings of the all-American dog. And my vehicle would be the densest form of poetry of all: the haiku. It didn't take long to run off a string.

Boss already told you about my first composition regarding the torment inflicted upon the American dog by paperboys. It was a revelation to find my frustrations take voice in my art. I soon turned my poetic voice to other feelings.

The American experience:

> Like America,
> I am a mixed-breed canine—
> I walk tall and proud.

Politics:

> In democracies
> Lineage doesn't matter.
> I am Melting Pot.

My personal heritage:

> My great-grandfather
> Chased big cats in Rhodesia.
> It is my birthright.

And it seemed as my skills grew, my courage to say the difficult things increased commensurately. Now, near the end of my life, I am honored (see the cycle?) with the publication of this volume of my work.

I would like to thank many for helping in this pro-duction: Boss and Mrs. Boss for always being behind me (especially when I slipped my collar and ran around the neighborhood); E.D., my sister-canine-in-crime, who composed many of these haiku with me; my human sisters Abbey, Sarah, and Maggie (especially Maggie, one of the finest dog whisperers I have ever met); my human brother, Dylan, who is a big fat jerk who never comes home to visit me anymore (Dylan, you're worse than a Siamese cat, and there's nothing worse.); my friends Hawk, Belle, and Harley up north

where a dog doesn't have to be chained up; my late friend, Tio, a Chicago Dalmatian who taught me the joys of pillows; and John Parsley, my editor, who read a copy of *Dog Daze* and "discovered" me. Thank you John.

Finally, I would like to thank every dog I have sniffed who has ever sniffed me back. You are my brothers and sisters and I write these for you, especially this haiku, conveyed in tones too high for a human to hear. For all dogs of all breeds everywhere:

! ! ! ! !
! ! ! ! ! ! !
! ! ! ! !

And that's the truth!
I am honored.

Humbly,
Honoré de Balzac, Dog Haikuist

14

Defense

They say the best defense is a strong offense.
Wrong. The best defense is a strong dog.

—Zac

The paperboy comes.

He wants to murder us all!

Bark! Bark! Bark! Bark! Bark!

I like to scare folks

Who walk obliviously.

I leap off the porch!

Calvin

When the Boss is gone

People walking by our door

Hear my mighty bark.

Bryce

If I could sniff out

That Osama bin Laden

I would bite him hard.

I bite the big dog.

He is so slow and clumsy.

I run away fast.

Jet

I am not afraid

Of you or anything but

The vacuum cleaner.

Dutch

Treats

They say integrity is its own reward.
Wrong. I like pig ears.

—E.D.

It is Halloween.

Small children ring our doorbell.

May I eat just one?

Belle

You act so angry

When I chew your leather shoe.

It was very good.

It is my nature

To be a chewing creature:

Shoes, belts, chairs, your hand.

Finlay

No matter what, the

Butter dish is off limits,

Even at midnight.

I don't feel so well.

I think I'll eat some tall grass.

Ack! Puke. That's better.

SPAM is good on bread

Hot or cold, but no damn good

In a garbage bag.

To the God, Hormel,

Thank you for sending us SPAM,

Food of the angels.

My picture outside.

Luscious food on the inside.

Not a doggy bag?

Biscuit

You are home! But you

Forget to give me a treat.

Where is the justice?

You are home! And you

Give me a giant pig ear.

I do puppydance.

Pi

Sleep

They say let sleeping dogs lie. Wrong.
Let sleeping dogs sleep. We never lie.
—Zac

You keep asking me

Why I climb up on the couch.

Because it is there.

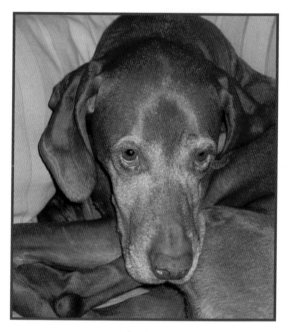

Jacko

Dog math is easy.

Eat: One-tenth, Poop: one-tenth, Sleep:

Whatever is left.

Dog-ku

All sleeping is good,

But on the couch is better.

On your bed is best.

When the Boss is gone

I sleep hard on the sofa.

She pretends I don't.

42

Tuesday

Napping is hard work.

Still, I must get up and eat,

Then I'll take a nap.

Puns

They say the pun is the lowest form of humor.
Wrong. Cats are the lowest form of humor.

—Zac

Father O'Brian

Spells "dog" backward but he too

Wears a stiff collar.

Hunter

Male dogs are called "dogs."

Female dogs are called "bitches."

Seems so judgmental.

I love my mother.

You call me son of a bitch

Like it's a bad thing.

Zeus

My verse is unique.

It is not "mere doggerel."

That critic has fleas.

The Iditarod

Makes but a single demand:

Press on doggedly.

Remes

Friendship

They say dogs are man's best friend. Wrong.
You have it backward.
—Zac

You speak so proudly

Of dog domestication.

We adopted *you*!

Schroeder

Dogs see black and white

But deep inside my dog heart

I'm your pal—true blue

Speckles

My tail goes spastic

When you come in from outside.

You've been gone minutes!

Morgan

If I had some thumbs

I could type my own haiku.

I wouldn't need you.

I smell the rabbit.

Tell the Boss to come help chase!

Bow-woooo, Bow-wooooo-oooooo.

60

Roxi

Dog-ku

On a summer day

When there's no one else around,

Fleas can be your friends.

Dog energy is

Contagious to my people.

Let's all jump and bark.

Brandy

Dog-ku

You got a dog door!

I have never been this free.

Out. In. Out. In. Out.

Dude, where's the Frisbee?

Throw it! Throw it! Throw it now!

Ruuuuuuuuuuuuuuuuuuuuun andbringitback.

Polly

Habits

They say old habits die hard. Wrong.
Bruce Willis dies hard. Old habits last forever.
—Zac

I don't need TV.

I can spend hours on the floor

Content with a bone.

Pal

Genes make me turn 'round

Three times before I lie down.

It's not OCD!

Roll over, lie down,

Sit, stay, heel, fetch, come, shake, speak.

What *else* do you want?

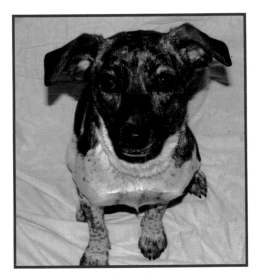

Biscuit

I don't shed that much.

Just enough to decorate

Your brand-new dress pants.

Maggie

I can catch my tail

Behind me now, behind me

It's still behind me.

Orson

Why no dog congress?

'Cuz we can't stop sniffing butts.

Oh wait! That's the same.

Do dogs play poker?

Only late at night, smoking

Pipes and fat cigars.

Moby

Eating

They say he's eating out of my hand. Wrong.
If it's a dog, he's eating out of your trash.

—Zac

THE RARE DOUBLE HAIKU

Dog food for breakfast.

Dog food for midday repast.

Dog food for dinner.

Dog food for night snack.

It's so dry and crunchable.

It's predictable.

Little Coyote

I found Nirvana.

It was right here all along

In the kitchen trash.

When you're at my house,

Boss and Mrs. Boss serve one

Kind of dog food—Mine!

Peaches

The Man is my boss

But Lady Boss makes my food.

My heart is more hers.

How long will I stay?

For food there is no end to

Canine loyalty.

Ricky

Dry dog food is hard.

Yet my old teeth are harder.

Canned food is for cats.

Cats (and Squirrels)

They say curiosity killed the cat.
Wrong. It was a dog.
—Zac

If that cat comes by

Just once when I'm off my chain

I'll make cat-burger.

Callie

Chasing terrorists

Is more fun than chasing cats,

But they taste much worse.

Those fuzzy squirrels

Have so far escaped my jaws

But some day . . . some day.

Sophie

In my twitching dreams

I'm a dog army of one.

Chasing hoards of cats.

Squirrels on the deck

Make me press my nose against

The doorwall and smear.

Sniper

You brought me a cat?

Why do you demote me? I'm

Deeply offended.

Dog-ku

Sonny

Beauty

They say beauty is only skin deep. Wrong.
I've seen some beautiful bones.
—Zac

My brand-new collar

Is bright red with white rhinestones.

I look marvelous.

Zoe

Dog-ku

I have been smelling

That dead rabbit for two days.

Ahhh . . . perfume for me.

100

When you yell at me

I am base, contemptible,

Worthless, wretched, wrong.

Who built this dog house?

It looks like a bordello.

It's embarrassing.

It's not that I'm fat—

Just short for my girth and weight.

Damn my little legs!

I am a girl dog.

Even I have been to school.

Some humans are fools.

Olive

In democracies

Lineage doesn't matter.

I am Melting Pot.

I don't fit my ears.

They flop around when I run.

I am still regal.

Dixie

Winter approaches.

Hair grows in my foot pads like

A frikkin' Hobbit.

Hygiene

They say cleanliness is next to godliness. Wrong.
There's your dyslexia acting up again.
—Zac

All day I sniff butts.

I come home to celebrate

By kissing your face.

109

Amy

My work is not done

Until every little child

Has a clean-licked face.

I am Snugglepup.

I love to love you better.

Let me lick your face.

Millie

A little baby!

It's so tiny and smelly.

I won't lick it much.

One thing I don't get.

Why do humans keep sitting

On the water bowl?

Petunia

Poop

They say their poop doesn't stink. Wrong.
All poop stinks, wonderfully!
—Zac

The door was open.

I distinctly smelled horses.

Manure to roll in!

Sarah

Just because I itch

Is no reason to be mean.

Don't call me "Scooter."

I mark many trees

I have an accurate aim.

Take that Scooby Doo!

Murphy Maximus Magoo

To all terrorists

Hiding in Afghanistan

I cock my hind leg.

Accidental poop

Left by your bedside with love.

Why do you step there?

My humans love me.

Every gift I give is dear.

They collect my poop.

Just because I'm small,

Don't dress me in people clothes.

I'll poop in your purse.

Ruby

Neighborhood

They say good fences make good neighbors. Wrong.
Dog biscuits make good neighbors.
—E.D.

I am not howling.

It is country music and

I'm singing along.

Tess

My great-grandfather

Chased big cats in Rhodesia.

It is my birthright.

Suburban dogs fly

In the SUV's front seat,

Head out the window!

Country dogs and trucks

Just go together like a

Redneck and his beer.

Cowboy dogs live well:

No dog walkers, cows to chase,

Miles between fences.

We New York dogs are

So urbane. All the rest are

Wolves from New Jersey.

Zoe

Vanity

They say Vanity, thy name is woman. Wrong.
Vanity thy name is Cockapoo.
—Zac

Yorkshire Terriers

Are here to teach you to share

Your heart and your lunch.

Sophie

I am nobly bred:

Specifically a Great-Chi-

Pinscher-Corgi-Hound.

I am a Bulldog.

Some say I look like Buddha

And Winston Churchill.

They call me Chow Chow.

I can't imagine why why.

Perhaps you know know.

I'm an Afghan Hound.

Still sporting this "Shag" haircut

Since the '70s.

I am a Shar-pei

And I can turn right around

Inside my own skin.

I am a Dachshund.

My middle is really really really really too long for this

poem but

My legs and head fit.

Lolita

An Irish Setter

Needs only the wind blowing

And a styling brush.

Collies are not gay.

We just know how to dress well

And walk with a prance.

Ruthie

I'm a Basset Hound.

I'm not as sad as I look.

I am quite mirthful.

I am a Yorkie.

No one could get away with

This hairdo but me.

140

Cecil

We Pugs evolved when

A small greyhound at top speed

Met the first shovel.

Like America,

I am mixed-breed canine—

I walk tall and proud.

142

Toughness

They say when the going gets tough, the tough get going. Wrong. These guys are tough, now get going.

—Zac

What is black and white

And full of vim and vigor?

Boston Terrier.

Madden

145

Dog-ku

I regard myself

As a white dog with black spots.

You may get it wrong.

Do dogs see color?

It doesn't really matter.

I am Dalmatian.

146

Though my brow's furrowed,

I am not worried at all.

I am a Bloodhound.

I'm a French Poodle.

I'm from a line of hunters.

I hate dog groomers.

German Shepherds bark

Much too loud for covert ops.

We growl low instead.

Bailey

I'm a Rottweiler.

I suffer from bad PR.

I need an agent.

What is black and brown

And looks good on a lawyer?

Doberman Pinscher.

Husky sled dogs know:

If you are not the lead dog,

The view doesn't change.

I'm Russian Wolfhound.

I grow weary of bahd jokes,

Like, why da long face?

They call me Husky.

Doesn't that mean I'm obese

In little boy pants?

Sex

They say opposite sex. Wrong.
There is sex and there is the opposite.
—Zac

Since you had me fixed,

Out of sheer embarrassment,

I squat when I pee.

Bo

Why do you squeal so,

When I only touch my nose

To your smelly place?

Girl dog sends out scents.

Wind travels great distances.

Boy dogs run for miles.

Sex

Patches

157

The old joke goes thus:

Why do boy dogs lick their balls?

It's because they can.

I've stopped humping legs,

But I can't contain myself

When your mother comes.

Choice

They say you are free to choose. Right. That's why
I invented these multiple-ending haiku. Pick
your favorite ending from the five choices.
—Zac

I just don't chase cars.

I feel no compunction to.

What if I caught one?

They don't have dog treats.

You can't eat a car.

You can't chew a car.

You can't hump a car.

Daphne

Are my legs too tall?

All the better to run down

Fundamentalists.

The conservatives.

Crazy liberals.

That dark blue pickup.

The Trick-or-Treaters.

Lila

My sense of smell is

five million times more than yours

and you say *I* stink?!

Now, about your breath . . .

Change your underwear.

Use deodorant.

But stinky cheese rules!

Rozzi

My feet are twitching.

I am running in my sleep,

Chasing terrorists.

Chasing Siamese.

Chasing slow squirrels.

Chasing fat rabbits.

Chasing my own tail.

Choice

Oliver

I like kitty cats.

Some of my best friends are cats.

Their brains are just small.

I chase them indoors.

They're fuzzy chew toys.

They taste like chicken.

Nah, I made that up.